# FatherCare

## *A Fresh Perspective on the Character of God*

## Jim Craddock

Scope Ministries International, Inc.

# INTRODUCTION

**Jesus came to reveal the Father!** (John 1:18; 10:30; 14:7, 9) All that He did, all that He said, all the miracles He performed demonstrated this amazing truth. It was in the humanity of our Lord Jesus that the Father found full and free expression as our Father. The life that Jesus lived and the death that He died were deliberate acts of revealing to humanity God the Father.

**In essence, Jesus was the Father here on earth!** Time and time again Jesus reiterated this truth—John 5:19-26; 8:18, 29, 42, 54; 10:30; 14:1-13. It is an inescapable fact that Jesus was on earth what the Father is in heaven. **God stepped out of heaven and became a man in the Person of our Lord Jesus Christ so that a Father's love and care could and would be demonstrated in person to heal and comfort those who were so desperately hurting.**

My own personal experience in counseling and ministering to literally thousands of Christians demonstrates that most believers hold an erroneous view of God as Father. What has happened is that they have based their own concept of the Father, not on the inspired Word of God, but on their own past relationship with their earthly fathers, good or bad. It is no small wonder then that the Church is weak and frail – **it knows not the Father!**

You don't trust a stranger, much less love him. To a great host of believers, the Father is some vague, spiritual being or some "cosmic policeman," who is ten million light years away. For all practical purposes He is a stranger to them. **How can we put any confidence in One we hardly know?** (See Psalm 9:10.) The answer is that we don't! Yet, James warns us of the emotional consequences when we lack confidence in God (James 1:6).

How can we break this belief system that has substituted an earthly father for the Heavenly Father? **The answer to this dilemma lies in the Person of our Lord Jesus Christ.** We must learn to see the Father in Him. As we do, the Holy Spirit will begin to change our own erroneous concepts of the Father into the correct one with all of the accompanying benefits.

Within the confines of our evangelical faith we have so sought to identify with Jesus that we have failed to see Him in His primary role, that of revealing the Father. Also, in an emphasis on seeking the Spirit and His gifts, we have also lost sight of the Father. **Jesus is not a substitute for the Father; He is the essence of the Father on earth.**

1

Paul wrote to the believers at Colossae:

**For in His physical body every attribute of the God-head continuously and permanently dwells.**

Colossians 2:9, author's paraphrase

Simply stated, this means that every attribute, every characteristic of the Father exists in the Person of our Lord Jesus Christ. All that the Father is, is in Jesus. **So, we must view Jesus as revealing the Father**. Otherwise, we will miss what he came to do – **UNVEIL THE FATHER.**

# FATHERCARE

Life is made up of relationships — some good, some bad — but all necessary. The Bible is God's inspired textbook on relationships. It is important to recognize the basic common denominator inherent in all relationships; that is, the foundational relationship from which all relationships originate, man's relationship to God, the Father/child relationship. It is this Father/child relationship that made Adam's interaction with God so unique, and it was the Father/child relationship that was lost at the Fall, thereby making man's life so desperate.

History shows us that men have always sought after God. Even from the earliest and most primitive of cultures, there has been a pattern of worship — of man's attempt to restore the lost Father/child relationship. However, it does not lie within the capabilities of man to restore this lost relationship. It has to be done by God. From God's perspective, the restoration of the Father/child relationship was so important that He stepped out of heaven in the Person of Jesus Christ to initiate and accomplish the process of restoring the Father/child relationship.

At the same time, the restoration of the Father/child relationship is so frighteningly threatening to Satan that he has made every attempt to hinder and confuse the process of that restoration (2 Corinthians 4:4). For a child of God to know God as Father brings that child into such intimacy with God, producing such worship of God and service for God, that the whole hierarchy of the evil one is threatened.

As we being this study, I want you to do an exercise. Write out a paragraph on who your father was to you as a person. Stop reading here and do that now:

_____

_____

_____

_____

_____

Believe it or not, years of having counselees do this exercise show that you have just described your concept of God as Father! That's right, most people transfer their experiential knowledge of their earthly fathers to the Heavenly Father. This is Satan's masterstroke of confusing the issue, and it is the reason why the vast majority of Christians have either an erroneous or, at the least, a very nebulous concept of God as their Father.

I once asked a missionary, who had come for counseling, to write out who her father was to her as a person. Later, I had her write out who the Father was to her as a Person. It stunned her to realize that she had written out basically the same thing for both. That was not an isolated case. I have found that most Christians have done this. Read a few of the comments that were received from hundreds of surveys taken with teens. The surveys asked them who their fathers were to them and who the Heavenly Father was to them as a Person. The surveys were taken at Christian conferences across the country and those surveyed indicated that they were Christians, active both in their churches and in the organization that sponsored the conferences.

Jennifer, age 15: *My father is a two-faced, irresponsible, mean S.O.B. Always perfect, nobody can ever do anything right. He is selfish and cruel. . . . There is no way I can picture God as my Father.*

Lee Ann, age 14: *My dad always seemed sort of far away. It's like he wants to love me, but he doesn't know how to. . . . God is sort of distant and hard to reach.*

Kristy, age 17: *Don't have and never knew my real father. . . . God is someone who sits on a white throne.*

Tammi, age 15: *My daddy loves me a lot, I think, but I am not sure 'cause my parents are divorced and I haven't seen my father in five years. . . . The Father to me is my protector and guide. Sometimes I feel like He doesn't love me as much as other people.*

Chris, age 19: *I hardly know my father. He has always been too busy working to spend time with me and the rest of the family. . . . My heavenly Father I think of similarly as my earthly father in that at times I think He's far off and too busy.*

I could multiply what was said by these young people hundreds of times by the adults who have come in for counseling. What I have found is a profound ignorance on the part of Christians about who God is as their Father. The result of this ignorance is far-reaching, affecting the Christian both spiritually and emotionally.

This phenomenon is particularly disturbing when we realize the importance that the Bible puts on knowing God. In fact, for us to know God as our Father is so critically important that God, in the Person of Jesus Christ, stepped out of heaven to reveal Him. The Bible demonstrates that all Jesus did, all that He said, was for this one single purpose of revealing God as our Father. What man had lost at the Fall — the Father/child relationship that existed between Adam and God — God was determined to restore through Jesus Christ!

**Studying how Christ revealed the Father is a study that can revolutionize your life, because it brings you into an intimacy with God as your Father that you have not experienced before.** The importance of this knowledge is attested to, not only in Scriptures, but by the great authors of Christendom. For example, J. I. Packer, in his book, *Knowing God*, says, "It is the most practical project anyone can engage in . . . Knowing about God is crucially important for the living of our lives."[1]

Kittle's *Theological Dictionary of the New Testament* says this:

> The glorifying of God's name is effected by Christ's work, and to this again it belongs that Jesus should reveal God's name to men as that of the Father. God's name is obscure to men; it is strange and general. But to those whom the Father has given Him, Jesus makes this name manifest, certain, and plain, so that it again acquires specific content: Father.[2]

I have stated over and over again, not only to counselees, but to Christian groups everywhere, that it is imperative for the Christian to know God as Father. A great deal of the Christian's emotional and spiritual problems can be laid at the feet of ignorance, ignorance of God and who He is as Father.

*Why Is It Important to Know God as Father?*

First, it is important to know God as Father because the Bible commands that we know God.

**. . . that the God of our Lord Jesus Christ, the Father of glory, may give to you a spirit of wisdom and of revelation in the knowledge of Him.**   Ephesians 1:17

---

[1] J. I. Packer, *Knowing God* (Downers Grove, Illinois: InterVarsity Press, 1973), p. 14.

[2] Gerhard Friedrich, ed., *Theological Dictionary of the New Testament*, Vol. 5 (Grand Rapids, Michigan: Wm. B. Eerdmans Publishing Co., 1967), p. 272.

**But from there you will seek the Lord your God, and you will find Him if you search for Him with all your heart and all your soul.**   Deuteronomy 4:29

**And He said to them, "You shall love the Lord your God with all your heart, and with all your soul, and with all your mind."**   Matthew 22:37

**And those that know Thy name will put their trust in Thee.**   Psalm 9:10a

**I have manifested Your name—I have revealed Your very Self, Your real Self—to the people You have given Me out of the world. They were Yours, and You gave them to Me, and they have obeyed and kept your Word.**   John 17:6 (Amplified)

To know God intimately, as God desires us to know Him, we need to know Him as Father. It is one thing to know God through His attributes, but it is quite another to know Him as Father. To know God only through His attributes tends toward a sterile, non-intimate relationship, while knowing Him as Father creates an awesome intimacy.

It is an astounding thing to read the Scripture and realize that God, the absolute Sovereign of the universe, desires that we should know Him, and that He should make it possible for us to do so. I repeat, **Christ's primary purpose of coming to this sin-ridden planet was to reveal God as Father, so that we, as his children, might enjoy that Father/child relationship that once existed between God and Adam.**

The very fact that God in the Person of Jesus did come to this earth to reveal the Father shows the importance God attaches to knowing Him. All that Jesus did and all that He said was to make God known as Father. By His life He gave content to the word "Father." It is interesting to note that the word "father" is used 418 times in the New Testament, and over half of the references, some 264, are of God as Father.

6

Jesus said:

**I and the Father are one.**                                    John 10:30

**If you had known Me, you would have known My
Father also; from now on you know Him, and have
seen Him. . . . He who has seen Me has seen the Father. . . . Do you not believe that I am in the Father,
and the Father is in Me? The words that I say to you
I do not speak on My own initiative, but the Father
abiding in Me does His works.**        John 14:7, 9b, 10

**But He answered them, "My Father is working until
now, and I Myself am working. . . . Truly, truly, I say
to you, the Son can do nothing of Himself, unless it
is something He sees the Father doing; for whatever
the Father does, these things the Son also does in
like manner. For the Father loves the Son, and shows
Him all things that He Himself is doing; and greater
works than these will He show Him that you may
marvel."**                                    John 5:17, 19-20

Not only are we commanded to know God, but second, knowing God as
Father is important for giving meaning to our lives. Packer puts it well:

> Knowing about God is crucially important for the living of
> our lives. As it would be cruel to an Amazonian tribesman to
> fly him to London, put him down without an explanation in
> Trafalgar Square and leave him, as one who knows nothing of
> English or England, to fend for himself, so we are cruel to
> ourselves if we try to live in this world without knowing
> about the God whose world it is and who runs it. The world
> becomes a strange, mad, painful place, and life in it a disap-
> pointing and unpleasant business, for those who do not know
> about God. Disregard the study of God, and you sentence
> yourself to stumble and blunder through life blindfolded, as it
> were, with no sense of direction and no understanding of

what surrounds you. This way you can waste your life and lose your soul.[3]

Third, it is important for the Christian to know God as Father for his emotional and spiritual well-being. A person cannot and will not trust a stranger. If God as Father is a stranger to us, for whatever the reason, we cannot and will not trust Him (Psalm 9:10). If we can't trust Him, we will doubt Him. And our doubts about God, while we try to live for God, produce a contradiction in our lives that creates tremendous emotional and spiritual stress (James 1:6). I have yet to have someone come in for counseling who was suffering from emotional stress and turmoil and had a good, Biblical concept of God as Father.

As you progress in this study, you will see how crucial it is to your spiritual development to know God as Father. In fact, as you begin to grasp this great truth of God as your Father, you will realize the tremendous spiritual and emotional benefits that accrue to the Christian who gains this knowledge.

### What Are the Benefits That Come From Knowing God as Father?

No relationship is more crucial to children than that of the parent/child relationship. In our culture, we sometimes forget how important the father/child relationship is. I have often stated that every daddy needs a little boy or little girl, and every little boy and little girl needs a daddy. What a loss when we realize that the average father spends approximately six minutes a day with his children. We live in a society that not only condones, but encourages, absentee fatherhood. What a refreshing and astounding difference it makes when we realize that God is our Father and is never absent, but always available to us every moment of every day.

Two passages of Scripture, among many others, confirm this fact of God's fatherhood to us:

> **A father of the fatherless, and a judge and protector of the widows, is God in His holy habitation.**
>
> Psalm 68:5 (Amplified)

> **And I will be a Father to you, and you shall be My sons and daughters, says the Lord Almighty.**
>
> 2 Corinthians 6:18 (Amplified)

---

[3] Packer, pp. 14-15.

Allow me to digress here for a moment to demonstrate how easily we have been deceived into erroneous thinking about God. In this passage from the Psalms, you will note that God selects two segments of society to specifically mention, widows and orphans. It is interesting to note that at the time of this writing, both widows and orphans were considered a detriment to society, a non-productive drain upon the culture.

In this passage, God is called a "judge." Now what image comes to your mind when you think of a judge? Normally, we see in our mind's eye an image of a judge behind his bench, dispensing justice from his perspective – and we feel guilty. Place this mental image of a judge over onto God and we come up with the concept of a "cosmic policeman" just waiting for us to step out of line.

However, God is *not* a judge in that sense. First, all judgment has been placed in Christ (John 5:22). Second, there is no condemnation to those who are in Christ (Romans 8:1). Third, all of our punishment was placed on Christ (Isaiah 53:5). Fourth, God doesn't remember our sins and transgression (Hebrews 10:17). Fifth, our transgression is forgiven and our sins covered (Psalm 32:1). So, if God is not a judge in the way we conceive of a judge, then how are we to define the way "judge" is used in Psalm 68:5?

The way that the word "judge" is used here is "one who evaluates worth"!!! Get this, for it is important – God as Judge is not one who condemns, but one who evaluates what is of worth. In this passage, He is evaluating as worthy the two segments of society which were considered worthless. **Therefore, God doesn't judge you in the sense of passing judgment unto condemnation, but He evaluates your absolute WORTHINESS!!!**

Now, what is a father? William Barclay says this:

> There are two English words which are closely connected, but whose meanings are widely different. There is the word "paternity" and the word "fatherhood." "Paternity" describes a relationship in which a father is responsible for the physical existence of a son; but, as far as paternity goes, it can be, and it not infrequently happens, that the father has never even set eyes on the son, and would not even recognize him if in later years he met him. "Fatherhood" describes an intimate, loving,

continuous relationship in which father and son grow closer

to each other every day.[4]

It is this "fatherhood that describes God's relationship to us. Thus, this is the greatest benefit of all in knowing God as Father — a continuing, growing intimacy with the Father.

However, this tends not to be our experience because on what basis do we build our concept of the Father? Humanly speaking, we establish father concepts through experiential relationships with our earthly fathers. Unfortunately, this produces erroneous concepts of a true father, because there is no absolutely perfect human father who can provide a role model for us.

Therefore, it is only through the Bible, our absolute standard of truth, that we can know what a father truly should be. It is the Bible that shows us, in the humanity of Jesus as He lived His life here on earth, the perfect role model as to what a true father is. It is there in the pages of Scripture that we see Jesus as the Father, a real Father in action.

What I am saying is that our normal father concepts tend to be erroneous, and it is only through the love and care of God, as we know Him as Father, that we can establish the proper concept of "father." It is in this Biblical dimension that we discover what a father truly is, that is, by seeing, in the Person of Jesus Christ, the Father at work here in our lives on earth!

A true father, a perfect father, a caring father is one who has the ability and desire to meet his children's deepest needs. And, what are our deepest needs? Let us discuss six of them:

- the need to worship
- the need to be loved and to belong
- the need for well-being
- the need to feel secure
- the need for approval
- the need for acceptance

---

[4] William Barclay, *The Daily Study Bible: The Letters of John and Jude* (Philadelphia: The Westminster Press, 1958), p. 87. Used by permission of St. Andrew Press.

## The Need to Worship

Most people would probably not list worship as one of their deeply felt needs, but it is man's most vital need because man was created for worship and to worship. Worship denied or wrongly expressed can and will cause wrong and/or harmful spiritual and emotional problems, as well as wrong behavior.

The word "worship" comes from the Anglo-Saxon word *weorthscipe*, which evolved into the word *worthship* and then into "worship." Worship is ascribing worth to someone or something. Man was not designed to live independent from God, but to commune intimately with, and totally depend upon, God. In order to live life as it was meant to be lived, to its fullest, man must ascribe to God His ascendant, infinite, absolute worth, His "first-place-ness." Man must worship. Without worship, we do not have God in His rightful place and, therefore, everything else in life is totally out of place. Right worship is ascribing to God His worth and worthiness.

It is through worship, right worship, that we come to know God and experience His love and care. Worship and intimacy are related. The greater the worship, the greater the intensity of intimacy. This is what our Father desires, an intimate relationship with us, His children. When His Spirit indwells us at our rebirth in Christ, He gives us the ability to rightly worship Him, to place Him in His rightful position, to honor Him and, therefore, to return to our deep dependence upon Him in every aspect of our lives – in other words, to be in an intimate, right relationship with our Father.

In a day and age where "self worth" is said to be man's basic need, we need to realize that worth, true worth – a true understanding of who we really are – can only come through worship, right worship – a true understanding of who God really is as the One of ultimate worth. In a sense, that is what this study is all about – to introduce you to who He really is: our loving heavenly Father, the One who meets all our needs out of His love, the One who is worthy of our worship, the only One who can fulfill our need to worship, because of His perfection and greatness and selflessness.

## The Need to Be Loved and to Belong

Probably no other word so characterizes Christianity as does the word "love." The profound mystic of the Christian faith is the overwhelming, overpowering, compelling unconditional love that flows from the pages of God's Word. It is a very basic, deeply felt need in all of our lives. We crave love – not a conditional love based on what we have or on what we are able to achieve, but an unconditional love, based upon who we are.

We need to love and be loved. It is the indispensable dynamic of our existence. And, our ability to love and be loved is directly related to our knowledge of God as our Father. The Bible says it best:

**We love, because He first loved us.**      1 John 4:19

Two words characterize our Father's love for us and to us. The first word is found in Ephesians 2:4, where the word "great" is associated with God's love for us. The second is found in 1 John 3:1, where the word "manner" (KJV) is associated with God's love.

The word "great" in the Greek is *polus* and signifies "much, many, or abundance." Here I think the word "magnificence" would best describe this love – a superabundance and overflowing of love from our Father to us. The word "manner" in the Greek is *potapos*, and Kenneth S. Wuest says, "The word speaks of something foreign. The translation could read, 'Behold what foreign kind of love the Father has bestowed upon us.'"[5] Actually, our words "exotic" or "incredible" would be suitable translations. What we are being told about our Father's love to us and for us is that it is **INCREDIBLY MAGNIFICENT!!!**

It is said that the love of God must have arms, and we are the arms through which the love of God is demonstrated. Let me share an incident that illustrates God's love for us. My wife, Doris, and I have five children – four boys and a girl. Our daughter is the youngest and the first girl in three generations of Craddocks. You can imagine the fuss made over this little piece of femininity when she pushed her way into this world. But the impact upon Danny, the youngest of the four boys, was something else. What do you do when you have three older brothers and, suddenly out of nowhere, comes a sister who steals the limelight? What you do is break the mold, and that is just what Danny did.

I could write a book about Danny. I will someday when I can safely change the names to protect the guilty. This boy could do more, get into more trouble, find the dirtiest mud hole, create more commotion than all the rest of our kids put together.

---

[5] Kenneth S. Wuest, *Word Studies in the Greek New Testament*, Vol. 4 (Grand Rapids, Michigan: Wm. B. Eerdmans Company, 1966), p. 142.

When Danny was a preschooler he was always going to marry one of the cute girls on our staff. He invariably had a crush on one or more of them, depending on who was the cutest and most responsive. One Sunday afternoon we had a rather formal tea to introduce new staff members. One young woman, Arlys, was a lovely brunette who came dressed in the prettiest, filmiest, whitest dress you ever saw. She was absolutely breathtaking.

As we adults were chatting, in came Danny, moving along with his dust cloud and looking like he just invented twelve new ways to incorporate dirt and mud into his four-year-old body. Just as he was about to head out the front door, out of the corner of his eye he caught a glimpse of this lovely girl in white and, in a second, he was up in her lap, hugging the life out of her.

I almost fainted. All I could see was a dirty, grimy little guy who was messing up the whitest dress in the room. But all Arlys could see was a little guy who needed loving, and she just loved on and hugged on him as though he were the only little guy in all the world.

God taught me something in that moment. We tend to look at ourselves as though we are the dirty, grimy guys, but God as our Father sees us only as little guys and gals who need lots of loving, and that is why His love is **INCREDIBLY MAGNIFICENT!**

Belonging to God allows us to fulfill the flip side of this need, that of belonging to others. God created us as social beings. He meant for us to relate to one another. In Genesis 2, God said that it wasn't good for man to be alone. The word "alone" in the Hebrew means "to be isolated." No one is an island unto himself. We need to belong.

If we are rightly related to God, enjoying the intimacy of right worship, then He becomes the prime mover in bringing other people into our lives to fulfill the need for belonging. How? He does this through the Church! – a family of like-minded people, born of His Spirit, enjoying oneness in His Spirit, learning to care for one another. Here is where the need to belong can be and should be met.

### The Need for Well-Being

Solomon wrote, "All of man's labor is for his mouth and yet the appetite is not satisfied" (Ecclesiastes 6:7). Man is driven to secure the basics of life – food, clothing and shelter. And once these are secured, man looks for emotional well-being.

However, our Lord made it quite clear in Matthew 6 that a sense of well-being comes, not through what we have or what we can get, but from who our Father is!

> . . . do not be anxious for your life, as to what you
> shall eat, or what you shall drink; nor for your
> body, as to what you shall put on. Is not life more
> than food, and the body than clothing? Look at the
> birds of the air, that they do not sow, neither do
> they reap, nor gather into barns, and yet your heav-
> enly Father feeds them. Are you not worth much
> more than they? . . . Observe how the lilies of the
> field grow; they do not toil nor do they spin, yet I
> say to you that even Solomon in all his glory did not
> clothe himself like one of these. But if God so arrays
> the grass of the field, which is alive today and to-
> morrow is thrown into the furnace, will He not
> much more do so for you . . .? Do not be anxious,
> then, saying, "What shall we eat?" or "What shall we
> drink?" or "With what shall we clothe ourselves?"
> For all these things the Gentiles eagerly seek; for
> your heavenly Father knows that you need all these
> things. But seek first His kingdom and His right-
> eousness; and all these things shall be added to you.
>
> Matthew 6:25-26, 28-33

We are to seek, first, His kingdom and His righteousness, and then all these things *will* be ours. Our Father promises to meet all of our needs, but only *He* can meet them. Our pursuit of them only leads to failure and frustration. As we relate to our Father, He opens our eyes to see His abundant provision, to see that our well-being is a need He eagerly desires to fulfill.

### The Need to Feel Secure

A father is one who provides security. **God our Father guarantees personal security.** This personal sense of security is affirmed and reinforced by the use of the term "Abba Father" in the Bible (Mark 14:36; Romans 8:15; Galatians 4:6). The word *abba* is a transliteration from an Aramaic word that signifies the first words a little baby says of its father. Our modern-day counterpart would be "da da." In other words, the best translation of the word *abba* would be "daddy"!! That is right. God is our "Daddy"! And I am not being disrespectful in the least.

The two words used in unison, "Abba Father," have great significance. The first demonstrates the childlike faith the believer is to have in his heavenly Father, followed by an adult appreciation of that childlike faith.

Let me share a personal chapter out of my own life that will illustrate the security that a daddy brings. When I was quite small, one of the "fun-est" things of all was to get a penny or two and go to Pinelli's corner grocery store and buy some candy. In those days a penny could go a long way toward corrupting a five-year-old addicted to candy. I can remember going to that store and yearningly looking over every piece of candy displayed in the case. I would pick and choose, drooling over what I couldn't afford, changing my mind constantly, asking dozens of questions, taking forever. (Of course, I was driving "old Man Pinelli" crazy in the process.)

However, there was a problem with getting my candy. To get to Pinelli's grocery store, I had to go up a block and over two blocks. This wasn't so bad, but situated at the strategic point midway between my house and Pinelli's was the biggest, ugliest four-foot bully you ever saw. He made the Incredible Hulk look like a ballet dancer. This bully and his buddy had a nasty habit of shaking me down for my pennies. (By the way, when you are three and a half feet tall, a four-foot bully looks immense.) Whenever this happened, I would return home blubbering about the threat to my life and the assault on my funds. I remember my dad telling me to stand up for my rights, but being of sound mind, and not necessarily suicidally depressed, I rejected that advice forthwith.

About the third time this degrading, depriving experience occurred, my dad told me that he would sneak up the alley, and if these two nemeses of my candy run interfered, he would handle them. Well, I can't begin to tell you the difference in my attitude. I was cock-o'-the- walk. I made faces at those two bullies. I flipped my pennies to let them know I was going to get some candy. In short, I was acutely obnoxious. However, I kept looking over my shoulder to make sure that my daddy was there. As long as I knew he was there, I had all the security in the world.

Of course, the moral to the story is that when we know God as our Father, as our *Abba*, our "Daddy," then we have that profound sense of personal security and safety. No matter what we face, the obstacles that lie in our paths, the struggles in our lives, our Father is there!!! He will never leave us nor forsake us! (Hebrews 13:5)

### The Need for Approval

Approval comes in many forms, and we all desire it. Everyone desperately seeks parental approval, and when it is not forthcoming, it creates real problems. As Christians we constantly seek God's approval. Jesus said, "Well done thou good and faithful servant" (Matthew 25:22). Proverbs says to give a pat on the back to whom it is due (Proverbs 3:27). Approval is a basic need of life. Through my counseling I have found that men who are younger than forty drive for success, while men over forty seek significance. Both are indicative of a need for approval. Since significance is so closely related to approval, let us look at it for a moment.

Have you ever thought what it is that gives significance? The early Greeks felt that it was determined by parentage. They felt a noble mind and virtue were inherited and could not be acquired.[6] In the rabbinical culture of Paul, his significance was based upon his being Jewish and a Pharisee, on belonging to the tribe of Benjamin and on his learning within the rabbinical schools (Philippians 3:5-6). In our day and age, significance is based upon performance, on what we are able to achieve, on credentials and on what we have. Notice in all these that significance is based on external factors, not internal ones.

Why is significance so important to us? Because it makes us "someone." It allows us to stand apart and above the crowd. It gives us the sense of approval we so deeply desire. But more importantly, in this mixed up, crazy world of ours, it is our way to try to gain a sense of worth. In the world system in which we operate, our approval and, hence, our significance, does not come from our inward sense of worth, but from our accomplishments achieved outwardly. The Biblical pattern is just the reverse.

The drive for approval is so strong that men will neglect their families, their health, all that they have, to gain it. Women will risk their happiness, their children, their futures, everything, to gain it. Why? Because we want so deeply to be somebody, to stand apart from the crowd, to leave an indelible mark on history, to stand approved before men. This drive explains why one survey I saw in a newspaper showed 82% of all American men were unhappy with their present employment and were considering changing jobs. A great number of men make a change as they

---

[6] Friedrich, Vol. 8, p. 2.

enter their forties because they feel it is their last chance to make an impact upon their world and, thus, their last change for gaining approval.

The Bible tells us that God gives His approval unconditionally in Christ! (Colossians 1:22) But how do we then, as Christians, gain a sense of this approval/significance? Is it through performance or achievement? Is it doing, is it having, or is it through some other means? Obviously, it is through God's means and not through man's efforts. Our Father is far more concerned with who we are than in what we do. In other words, as far as the Bible is concerned, approval and significance is related to **BEING**, not doing. Real, lasting approval comes from a relationship with the Father that insures us that we are His children.

I have mentioned some aspects of what a father is, but there is another factor which would normally go without saying, and that is that a father is one who has children. Really profound, you say! Yes, it is when you consider who the Father is and what that makes us as His children. Under the inspiration of the Holy Spirit, Paul quoted to the Corinthians an astounding truth from 2 Samuel:

> **And I will be a Father to you, and you shall be My sons and daughters, says the Lord Almighty.**
>
> 2 Corinthians 6:18 (Amplified)

God, the almighty, majestic God of the universe is our Father!!! This means that we really do have a Father who is **consistent**, who is **kind** and **caring**, **loving** and **thoughtful**. We have a Father who **cherishes** us, who is happy when we are happy, sad when we are sad. He is a Father who brings immeasurable fullness into our lives.

On what basis can I as a Christian really know that I am truly a child of God? How can I have that personal security and knowledge that God accepts me and saves me once for all, for all eternity – that I have the ultimate approval? The assurance that we need can be summed up in one Biblical word, **"ADOPTION"**! However, it is important that you realize that the Biblical concept of adoption is totally different from our idea of adoption today. Our use of the word "adoption" involves children, while the Biblical use of the word involves adults. In other words, we are adopted by God as adult sons and daughters, not just as small children.

The word "adoption" in the Greek is *huiothesias* and is used only five times in the New Testament. This kind of adoption was peculiar to the Romans and was unknown to either the Greek or Jew.[7] It spells out in detail what God has in mind when he uses it in regard to us. William Barclay gives us a most graphic description of Roman adoption in his commentary on Romans 8:12-17.

It is only when we understand how serious and complicated a step Roman adoption was that we really understand the depth of meaning of this passage. Roman adoption was always rendered more serious and more difficult by the Roman *patria potestas*. The *patria potestas* was the father's absolute power over his family; that power was absolute; it was actually the power of absolute disposal and control, and in the early days it was actually the power of life and death. In regard to his father, a Roman son never came of age. No matter how old he was, he was still under the *patria potestas*, in the absolute possession, and under the absolute control, of his father. Obviously this made adoption into another family a very difficult and a very serious step. In adoption a person had to pass from one *patria potestas* to another. He had to pass out of the possession and control of one father into the equally absolute possession and control of another. There were two steps. The first was known as *mancipatio*, and it was carried out by a symbolic sale, in which copper and scales were symbolically used. Three times the symbolism of sale was carried out. Twice the father symbolically sold his son, and twice he bought him back; and the third time he did not buy him back, and thus the *patria potestas* was held to be broken. After the sale there followed a ceremony called *vindicatio*. The adopting father went to the *praetor*, one of the Roman magistrates, and presented a legal case for the transference of the person to be adopted in his *patria potestas*. When all this was completed then the adoption was complete. Clearly this was a serious and impressive step.

But it is the consequences of adoption which are most significant for the picture that is in Paul's mind. There were four

---

[7] Wuest, Vol. 1, p. 134.

main consequences. (i) The adopted person lost all rights in his old family, and gained all the rights of a fully legitimate son in his new family. In the most literal sense, and the most binding legal way, he got a new father. (ii) It followed that he became heir to his new father's estate. Even if other sons were afterwards born, who were real blood relations, it did not affect his rights. He was inalienably co-heir with them. (iii) In law, the old life of the adopted person was completely wiped out. For instance, legally all debts were canceled; they were wiped out as if they had never been. The adopted person was regarded as a new person entering into a new life with which the past had nothing to do. (iv) In the eyes of the law the adopted person was literally and absolutely the son of his new father.

That is what Paul is thinking of. He uses still another picture from Roman adoption. He says that God's Spirit witnesses with our spirit that we really are the children of God. The adoption ceremony was carried out in the presence of seven witnesses. Now, suppose the adopting father died, and then suppose that there was some dispute about the right of the adopted son to inherit, one or more of the seven original witnesses stepped forward and swore that the adoption was genuine and true. Thus the right of the adopted person was guaranteed and he entered into his inheritance. So, Paul is saying, it is the Holy Spirit Himself who is the witness to our adoption into the family of God.

We see then that every step of Roman adoption was meaningful in the mind of Paul when he transferred the picture of adoption into the family of God. Once we were in absolute possession of sin, in absolute control of our own sinful nature; but God, in His mercy, has brought us into absolute possession of Himself. The old life has no more rights over us; God has an absolute right. The past is canceled; the debts of the past are wiped out; we begin again a new life, a life with God. We become heirs of all the riches of God. If that is so, we become joint-heirs with Jesus Christ, God's own Son. That which Christ inherited, and inherits, we also inherit.

It was Paul's picture that when a man became a Christian he entered into the very family of God. He did nothing to earn it; he did nothing to deserve it; God, the great Father in His amazing love and mercy, has taken the lost, helpless, poverty-stricken, debt-laden sinner and adopted him into His own family, so that the debts are canceled and the unearned love and glory inherited.[8]

What Biblical adoption means is that, as a Christian, you are a chosen child of God and God is your Father. He has adopted you as a son or daughter into His family. It means that nothing can ever change that fact — nothing you can do or ever will do changes the fact that you are an adopted child of God. You are indelibly written in the Lamb's book of life forever and ever. And because you are adopted, you are destined to an eternity with the greatest Father in all the universe.

What does this have to do with approval? Medical science tells us that we are the sum total of our parents' genes, a blending of the two. To a large degree, I am what they are. So it is with the new birth. I become one with my Father in heaven. I become in reality an image-bearer, having been created in the image of God. What greater approval and significance can there be than to realize that, as Christians, we are children of the Most High and Holy God? What is so amazing is that God gives so unconditionally — His love, His care and, of course, His approval.

One time, after I led a Bible study, a young mother approached me and requested to see me for counseling. Later, in the privacy of my office, she shared with me about a childhood with a demanding, demeaning father. No matter what she did, it was never good enough. She could never quite measure up to her father's expectations. Even though her father had been dead for a number of years, she was still in a desperate search for his approval.

I wish this were an isolated case, but it isn't. One of the strongest drives of a person's life is for parental approval. And, the higher the expectations of the parent, the harder it is to gain a sense of his or her approval.

---

[8] William Barclay, *The Daily Study Bible: The Letter to the Romans* (Philadelphia: The Westminster Press, 1958), p. 109-112. Used by permission of St. Andrew Press.

What makes it all so hard is that God created man to be loved, accepted, approved, and understood unconditionally. I mean by this that there is innately in us the expectation and need to be received unconditionally. However, we are born into a world system that receives no one unconditionally, but only conditionally based on what a person is able to do, achieve or have. Every person born into this world discovers that there is a direct contradiction between the desire to be received unconditionally and the world's refusal to honor that need. This contradiction produces enormous stress, especially in light of the tremendous drive that we all have for approval.

At the Fall, man's concept of God was shattered and replaced with an erroneous mindset. Man then had no absolute basis of worth, so his own identity was shattered. Because man had no basis of unconditional worth, he had to compensate. He did this by adopting a compensating system of self-imposed standards, which would allow him to gain conditionally what was denied him unconditionally. He tried to gain worth and significance through his performance rather than in his being as was God's original plan before sin entered into the picture.

What happens is that a person is born into a world system with no basis of unconditional worth. This guarantees a poor identity or poor self-image. Therefore, a person doesn't consider himself worthy enough to receive anything unconditionally. Still, those inward drives and needs for approval must be satisfied, so we all opt for a compensating system of self-imposed rules and regulations, standards by which we can measure ourselves and gain the "strokes" we feel we need.

I call this compensating system the "Torah Syndrome." In Hebrew, *torah* means "the embodiment of the law." What we do is impose upon ourselves a standard or "law" to gain "strokes." In other words, if I don't get what I need unconditionally, I impose upon myself a standard which, if I keep it, can give me conditionally what I desire emotionally. For example, I might decide, "If I make straight A's, then I'll know I'm worthy." Usually we have an elaborate set of such rules for ourselves. They enable us to measure our worth through performance.

Reflect back for a moment to your own childhood. Think of the system you adopted to gain approval from your parents. What did you do to be thought of as a good little boy or girl? Every family has their limits and standards. Approval comes, not from who we are, but from our ability to meet these limits and standards. If you do "this and this and this," then you receive the approval you are looking for. This forces you into a performance bias, which sets the stage for the "Torah Syndrome" you create for yourself as an adult.

The moment we impose upon ourselves standards to gain approval, we deny the innate desire for unconditional approval and acceptance. Therefore, we are doomed to failure. We can never do enough, achieve enough, have enough to satisfy that longing. We keep thinking that more standards will provide that sense of approval, but what we really want is *unconditional* approval. Getting caught up in this "Torah Syndrome" causes many Christians to suffer nervous breakdowns.

However, our Father, who created us to be received unconditionally, does receive us unconditionally. His approval is given on the basis of who He has made us to be in Christ, not on the basis of what we do. He loves us, he accepts us, he approves of us as His children.

A story, again involving Danny, my youngest son, demonstrates this unconditional receiving. Danny was accident-prone. Twice, firemen in large ladder trucks had to rescue him from the heights of enormous trees. His body is riddled with the scars from hundreds of stitches. When he was two and a half, it took seven stitches to repair his head when he got too curious about the neighbor digging out a cistern. At three, he cut his finger off in a car door. (Thankfully, a surgeon restored it.) When he was four, it took over a hundred stitches to repair a leg cut open when he fell. What all this did was to build into Danny a healthy fear of anyone in a white smock!

So, when Danny began to complain of a toothache, I took him to a dentist friend of mine; but when Danny saw the white smock, he figured that here was more pain. He fought for his life. In about fifteen minutes, my friend came out and asked me to take Danny somewhere else (like to a home for incorrigible children).

I had another friend named Charley Brown (really), who was a dentist. Charley told me that he could handle Danny. He said he had had twenty hours of child psychology and this was a good opportunity to put into practice what he had learned.

When we arrived at Charley's office, I offered to help out, but it was felt that I would be more of a hindrance than a help. So, I sat in the foyer listening to the shouts, cries, thudding, etc., until finally Charley came out and asked me to come in. It seemed that when he held Danny's arms with one hand and the drill with the other, with the nurse holding Danny's feet, there was no way to get Danny to open his mouth. Here I am afraid that I destroyed in twenty minutes twenty hours of child psychology. I took off my belt (I refer to this as B-therapy) and told Danny if he didn't open his mouth, I would apply B-therapy.

For four sessions, Charley labored with Danny, along with "the belt and I," through all the strugglings, cryings and fightings that only a pain-enlightened four year old can produce. Finally, when it was all through, we were seated in Charley's office when Charley came in, sat down and, without a word, caught Danny up and hugged and loved on him and said, "Danny, I love you!"

Now Danny knew that he had done nothing to deserve this kind of unconditional approval. In fact, if he had gotten what he deserved, he wouldn't nor couldn't sit down for a week. But all the way home, Danny kept saying over and over again to me, "Daddy, that man really loved me!"

The moral of this story is that we have done nothing to deserve God's unconditional love or approval, but He gives it anyway, not on the basis of what we have or haven't done, but on the basis of His Beloved Son. You can't earn God's approval. All of your little systems to gain God's "strokes" won't work with Him. He gives you His approval unconditionally. You simply are to receive it in faith! We could say then with Packer:

> There is tremendous relief in knowing that His love for me is
> utterly realistic, based at every point on prior knowledge of
> the worst about me, so that nothing I can do will disillusion
> Him about me.[9]

The Father knows it all, and He gives you His approval still.

### The Need for Acceptance

Approval and acceptance are very closely related. If we feel approved, we will feel accepted. Unfortunately, many Christians do not feel approved or accepted by God. This happened in my case. As a new Christian, I was taught that God didn't love me, but rather he loved the Christ in me. In fact, I was told by many a preacher that there was no good thing in me and that, because of sin, God could only stand to look at me through "rose-colored glasses." The rose-colored glasses represented the blood of the Lord Jesus. All of this really tended to reinforce my own poor self-image.

What a tragedy that a lie of the pit is preached as though it were the truth of heaven. How ridiculous! God doesn't love the Christ in me. **He loves me!** Of

---

[9] Packer, p. 41.

course, He loves His Son. That isn't even the issue. The issue is that He loves me, He accepts me unconditionally. It isn't the Christ in me that makes me acceptable to God. It is what Christ did on the cross that makes me acceptable to Him. And God, my Father, accepts me, Jim Craddock, with all my hang-ups, with all my sins, with all my idiosyncrasies, as a person, unconditionally.

For years, as a Christian involved in Christian work, I never believed that God could or would accept me unconditionally. How could He? There was no good thing in me. Well-meaning men did me and many, many others a great disservice by telling me this. But, it was through the greatest crisis of my life up to that time that I discovered the truth that was to change my life.

In the ministry I was in, tremendous animosity had arisen between the president and the top directors, of which I was one. On our part, there was an unreasonable reaction to the productivity demands and a frustration over what seemed to us a dictatorial style of leadership. On the president's part, there was a lack of understanding and communication. During those tense, almost unbearable hours, as charge and countercharge were made and many unfortunate statements were said, I was struggling with my own deepened sense of inadequacy and failure. I felt that I couldn't bear what was happening to the ministry I loved and the people I respected.

During one of the breaks in the meetings, when everything seemed so hopeless, one of the directors turned to the president of the organization and said, "You know, I haven't loved you unconditionally as I should, and I just now realized it. Will you forgive me?" This was the breaking point, for from that moment on, God had the victory.

But for me, in that moment, it suddenly dawned on me that God loved me unconditionally – not the Christ in me. It was not what I was able to do for Him, but that He loved me as me. He loved me as a person, not the Christ in me, but Jim Craddock with all of his weaknesses.

It took time, but I came to experience personally His unconditional acceptance. What a relief it was not to have to struggle for his acceptance or His love and approval, but just to receive them by faith. How great it was and is to be unconditionally loved and accepted by the Father in heaven.

### Relationship

I mentioned that a father is one who has children and meets the needs of those children, but there is another facet of fatherhood which I want to develop, and it is crucially important to both father and child. It is that of relationship – a relationship involving three factors: a **continuing** relationship, a **growing** relationship and an **intimate** relationship.

A true father/child relationship is always a **continuing** relationship. We see this in the parable of the prodigal son (Luke 15:11-32). Nothing that the son did affected the relationship of the father to the erring son. The father maintained a continuous relationship with the son. What this parable means to us is that our Father maintains a continuous relationship with us. Nothing can affect it. This is important because every child needs a parent that remains unchangeable even in the face of a changeable child. As a father, I am not to respond in kind to my children's outbursts or inconsistent behavior. I am to be unmovable and unchangeable in my love. Unfortunately, I fall short of this, but my Father in heaven does not! (However, it is important to remember that although nothing affects God's relation to us, sin in our lives can and will affect *our* relation with Him.)

If I am faithless, He is faithful (2 Timothy 2:13). If I am impossible, he is kind. If I am angry with Him, He is patient. In other words, what I need desperately is the security of a Father whose attitude of love, kindness, acceptance and approval is not subject to the whims of vacillating emotions. And we do have a Father who is consistent in His relationship with us.

Having had my own teenaged daughter, I have struggled with thoughts and feelings about what I would do if she were immoral and ended up pregnant out of wedlock. Consequently, when the daughter of a friend of mine bore a child out of wedlock, I asked him how he had handled the obviously difficult and painful situation. His reply was, "I loved her as my daughter before this happened, and I love her as my daughter now that it has happened." He had a continuing relationship with his daughter that transcended her behavior.

Don't get me wrong. He didn't condone what she had done. He hated the sin, but he allowed nothing to affect his relationship with his daughter. He deeply loved her and the child she bore. This is illustrative of God's continuing relationship with us. We are his children by His choice, not ours, and having made that choice, He allows nothing to destroy it!

Not only is our relationship with our heavenly Father a continuing one, it must be a **growing** one – one that grows deeper every day. There is one relationship that we have with our children as babies and quite another as they enter into puberty. When my children were small, we packed them everywhere. We couldn't afford babysitters, so we had to. But then, that wasn't really a problem. We loved showing them off. As they grew older, we would take them with us whether they wanted to or not. We would carefully instruct them on what to do, how to act, to be polite, etc. But when the time came for them to be perfect little men and women, they would allow their mother's genetic side to come through and blow the whole thing!

As my children became young adults, it was a different story. By then my relationship with them had taken on new dimensions. When the kids were in junior high and high school, I would have luncheon dates with them. Once a week we would have a date, and off we would go to scarf down a hamburger and a coke. (They referred to this as a "gut-bomb and a belly-wash.") This gave us time to talk, more like adults.

Now that they are adults, my children and I relate as adults. Our relationship has been one that has continued to grow. Unfortunately, this is not true of all father/child relationships. I'll never forget one young lady who approached me after a meeting in a sorority house where I'd spoken. My topic had been on the father/child relationship. She came up afterwards and said, "My father deserted our family when I was two, and I made up my mind that I didn't need a daddy!" Then she dissolved into tears and cried on my shoulder over and over again, "Oh, but I do need a daddy, I do need a daddy!"

Our Father guarantees us a **continuing** relationship with Him, but the **growth** of that relationship is a great deal dependent upon us. In his book, *Enjoying Intimacy With God*, J. Oswald Sanders graphically describes the various positions of the disciples with Christ:

> Each of the disciples was as close to Jesus as he chose to be, for the Son of God had no favorites. . . . It is a sobering thought that we too are as close to Christ as we really choose to be.[10]

Out of this continuing and growing relationship with our Father, there develops **intimacy**. This intimacy with the Father is not a luxury, but a necessity for our well-being. The whole purpose of this study is to enable you to develop an ever deepening intimacy with the Father as you come to know Him through the Person of His Son, Jesus Christ.

---

[10] J. Oswald Sanders, *Enjoying Intimacy With God* (Chicago: Moody Publishers, 1980), pp. 19-20.

26

The question is, just how badly do you want this intimacy? Again, quoting from Mr. Sanders, "It would seem that admission to the inner circle of deepening intimacy with God is the outcome of **deep desire**. Only those who count such intimacy a prize worth sacrificing anything else for are likely to attain it."[11] (emphasis mine)

Isn't it astounding that our Father would make such provision for this type of relationship with us, His children? As I said previously concerning His love for us, and I say it again, His love-relationship with us is **<u>INCREDIBLY MAGNIFI-CENT!!!</u>**

What then is a father? One who begets children, who raises and nourishes them, who meets their needs, and who encourages an ever growing, continuing relationship with them. But, more than all of this, a father is one who loves his children dearly and who tenderly watches over them, cares for them, understands them, talks with them, listens to them, and is vitally concerned for them. This is *our* heavenly Father.

## *Beginnings*

Before we enter into the practical phase of our study, let me share with you how this particular study came about. It all began with a phone call from a tearful young wife and mother (I'll call her Pat), who was requesting an appointment. Because she was so emotionally upset, I set an appointment for the next morning. Pat arrived early, and as we began our discussion, she poured out her feelings. Having grown up in the church, she understood what it meant to be a committed Christian. In the course of our conversation, she related that, although her grandfather had been a pastor and the church an integral part of her family life, her father had divorced her mother when Pat was quite young. This had caused a lot of disillusionment and bitterness on her part.

In the course of our counseling, I had Pat write out who God was to her as a person. She wrote that God was an all powerful, all loving, all knowing being. Later, for some reason, I had her write out who the heavenly Father was to her as a person. I was astounded to see that she had written out that, to her, the Father was a liar, a thief and a sneak.

I pointed out the contradiction to Pat, and we worked through his misconception. But my curiosity was aroused, so I began to ask a number of people the

---

[11] Ibid., p. 20.

same two questions. Far too often, they did just what this young woman had done, in that they described two different persons! They had one concept of God as God and another of God as Father.

Then I began having counselees write out who their fathers were to them as a person and who the Father was to them as a person. Again, I was astonished to find that almost everyone was saying the same thing about two different persons. It was obvious that they were patterning their concept of God as Father after their experience with their earthly fathers. Two conclusions seemed to emerge: (1) many Christians are "double minded" as it concerns God as God and God as Father, and (2) most Christians pattern their concept of God after their earthly fathers.

The next stage of my own discovery of this great truth of knowing God as Father came as I was speaking to a class of young ladies at Louisiana State University. During some interaction before my evangelistic presentation, I discovered that most of the class was made up of fairly conservative Jewish girls. However, although my message was about Christ, they proved a very attentive and appreciative audience.

Following the class, I was approached by one of the Jewish girls who told me that, if I was willing to listen, she could tell me how I could become world famous. Of course, anytime a cute young lady wants to tell me how to become world famous, I will listen. So, I told her that I would buy her a Coke and off we went to a quiet part of the student union. We had no sooner seated ourselves than she stated, "What you have to say is not only interesting, but imperative for people to hear. However, by mentioning the name of Jesus you cause people to turn off." She then very earnestly begged me to no longer speak of Jesus, but only of God.

This led to a lively discussion – she talking of God and I of Christ. But she had a peculiar habit that was very disturbing to me. Whenever she spoke of God, great tears would come to her eyes. Her sense of the awesomeness of God was amazing. She seemed to have an awareness of God that was missing from my life. Of course, I had Christ, but I came away from that encounter knowing that I did not know God in the way that I ought.

### New Dimensions

The more I thought about God as my Father, the more I realized that I really did not know Him as a Father. My intimacy was with the Son. I knew Jesus. I had served Him for years, but I remained ignorant of the Father.

It was during this time of new awareness about God as Father that I received word that my father was dying. I rushed to his bedside, but he had only hours to live. During the confusion of the next few days, I was too busy to think much about this death, but when I caught my plane to go to my next conference speaking engagement, I contemplated my relationship with my father. The thought kept going over and over again in my mind, "I never really knew him!" My father was a good man, a provider. He had his problems, including a bout with alcoholism, but he had "taken the cure" and hadn't had a drink in 25 years. As I thought of the good times and the bad times, I thought over and over, "I never knew the man."

Suddenly, it occurred to me that I had the same feelings about God the Father. I really didn't know Him as Father. It all seemed to come together, for I too had projected the image of my earthly father onto my heavenly Father. When I returned home, I began to search through the Psalms, for the first time seeking out God as my Father. I reveled in the great and graphic descriptions of the majesty of God found in Scripture. I read every book that I could get my hands on concerning God. I studied His attributes, then His names. It was a thrilling experience.

But the greatest thrill of all was when I discovered that Jesus had come to reveal the Father. This was His primary purpose in coming to this sin-ridden planet. By studying the life of Christ, I could see in detail the Father at work here on earth. In Jesus I could see all the characteristics of the perfect Father. It was in Jesus loving that I saw a loving Father. It was in Jesus caring that I saw a caring Father. It was in Jesus approving that I experienced a Father's approval. It was in Jesus' kindness that I saw a kind Father. It was in Jesus' gentleness that I saw a gentle Father. It was in Jesus' acceptance that I knew a Father's understanding. It was in Jesus' security that I knew the security of a Father. It was in a patient Jesus that I saw a patient Father. It was in Jesus that my knowledge of the Father began to become complete.

Let me illustrate this from Scripture. Take the marriage feast at Cana (John 2:1-10). You are familiar with the story. Jesus' mother was in charge of the wedding. She had planned it, executed it, and was obviously anxious over it. Then the unexpected occurred and they were running out of wine. This could have been disastrous. It would have embarrassed the bride and groom and humiliated Mary. But was Jesus going to let this happen? Would he allow the wedding feast to be spoiled and His mother to suffer the indignity of failing in her preparations for the feast? Of course not. He cared! He cared even for the insignificant things in the lives of people. This was the Father at work. The Father cares. Jesus made this very plain in John 5:19-23.

Take the young man born blind (John 9). People were calloused in that culture. To be born blind could only mean that either you or your parents were under God's judgment. This meant a life of total rejection and ridicule, a life of begging, of groveling in the dirt for every measly morsel. Even the disciples were caught up in this mindset.

Why did Jesus heal the young man? To show His own greatness, to give vent to his deity? Of course not! When Jesus looked at that young man, he didn't see a dirty, filthy beggar. He didn't see a man destined to live out his life under the supposed judgment of God. What He saw was a young man who wanted desperately to be able to see. It was the caring Father in the Person of Jesus who cared enough for that young man that He healed him of his affliction. It was the Father at work, a caring, loving Father.

Take the leper in Matthew 8. If you know anything about leprosy, you will know that it is one of the most horrible of diseases known to mankind. Even today, if a person contracts leprosy, he becomes an instant outcast. In the time and culture of Jesus, leprosy was considered a most dreaded disease, one to be greatly feared lest it spread. Being a leper meant a life of living death, outcast from any normal type of life, doomed to eke out an existence with other lepers, fighting desperately for life while scavenging for food among garbage dumps. A leper knew nothing of what it meant just to talk with someone, to be held and touched, to have someone look at him without flinching. A leper could not enter the city nor attend the synagogue. Lepers were ostracized from their own families. For a leper to approach a normal, healthy person meant instant death through stoning.

Yet, here in Scripture we are witness to an incredible event. Driven by desperation, fearing life more than death, a leper walks right up to Jesus. The leper could have been stoned for this. He falls at Jesus' feet and pleads for healing. And what did our Lord do? An incredible thing! He actually reached out and touched that loathsome leper. He put His great arms around the filthy leper and held him and told him, "I will cleanse you! I will heal you!" I wonder, in that pregnant moment, with all the bystanders gaping aghast, what it meant for that man to feel those strong arms of Jesus around him and to hear that soothing, gentle, loving voice say, "I will heal you!"

Why did Jesus do such a thing? Because the Father cared! It was the Father at work in Jesus. When He looked at that leper, He didn't see the loathsome, despicable, dross of human society. He saw a man intensely desperate to be healed, to be normal. Jesus cared – the Father cares!

And what about the little street prostitute who invaded the private garden party of Simon the Pharisee (Luke 7:36-50)? What a potentially embarrassing moment. Here was Jesus, known for His purity and holiness, reclining in the open courtyard of Simon's house. Not only were there guests, but the townspeople were crowded around the courtyard walls waiting to listen to this young teacher who was stirring up all the people. What would they think? I wonder what the reaction would be today if a well-known prostitute ran up to a famous preacher during Sunday services and threw herself at his feet. He would probably be run out of town.

Notice Jesus' amazing reaction. He allows this young woman to wash His feet with her tears and to dry them with her hair. He actually allows her to anoint Him with perfume. Does He leap up in indignation? No. Does He scream at her for her actions? No. Does He cast her out? No. What does He do? He receives her. He doesn't humiliate her or reject her. He is protecting her, a common street prostitute! Why? Because the Father is at work. Now, you can see why I call the love of God the Father **INCREDIBLY MAGNIFICENT!!!**

We know the Father as our own Father through our Lord Jesus! **It is as we see Jesus as a Father that we come to know the Father!**

> **O taste and see that the Lord is good; how blessed is the man who takes refuge in Him!** Psalm 34:8

This relationship with God as Father is two-sided. It was initiated by Him, carried on by Him, but it demands a response on our part. As to God's part, Packer puts it well:

> What matters supremely, therefore, is not, in the last analysis, the fact that I know God, but the larger fact which underlies it – the fact that *He knows me*. I am graven on the palms of His hands; I am never out of His mind. All my knowledge of Him depends on His sustained initiative in knowing me. I

know Him because He first knew me and continues to know me.[12]

And to man's part, Sanders says:

> Both Scripture and experience teach that it is we, not God, who determine the degree of intimacy with Him that we enjoy. We are at this moment as close to God as we really choose to be.[13]

The Bible calls God's part of the relationship "grace," and the part which is ours is faith." Grace has been called the "divine adequacy." Faith is the human response to our Father's adequacy. As we grow in awareness of His adequacy, we grow in our experience of the love and care and peace of the Father.

Why is it important for us to see the Father in Jesus? Mainly because we are told by Jesus that the Father is spirit (John 4:24), but we can't identify with spirit. Being flesh and blood, we only relate with flesh and blood. How then was the Father to reveal Himself? Obviously, through the Son. Therefore, to know God as Father, you must know Him as such through our Lord Jesus!

### Reparenting

There are nine Bible studies in the application section of this booklet. These are to help in a "reprogramming" or a "reparenting" process to replace wrong ideas about God with right ideas about God. These wrong ideas about God have been programmed into us over the years through experiential relationships with our earthly fathers and form a basic part of what we call our "belief system."

Our "belief system" is everything we believe about God, about ourselves, about others and about the world around us. Unfortunately, much of our "belief system" is erroneous; thus, it needs to be changed. God's means of changing our "belief systems" is through the **renewing of the mind** (Romans 12:2). In regard to how we view God as Father, our term "reparenting" is used interchangeable with "renewing of the mind." This process of renewing or reparenting consists of two basic elements: (1) the **putting off** of the wrong ideas about God and (2) the **putting on** of the right ideas about God.

This "putting off" and "putting on" process takes time. This is why the Bible studies at the end of this booklet are designed to be done over a number of weeks.

---

[12] Packer, p. 41.
[13] Sanders, pp. 13-14.

You should schedule your time to spend a minimum of two weeks on each of the studies.

You will note that there are two sections in the back of this booklet: the workbook section and the application section. The workbook section involves a Bible study consisting of questions and answers. Look up the verse related to the question and then write out the answer in the space provided. It would be helpful to also read the passages of scripture both before and after the verse being cited.

The application section is a combination of Scripture memory and prayer. This section has two parts. First, there is a "Relationship Test," which covers ninety characteristics of the Father. Each group of ten characteristics is correlated with a Bible study page in the second part of the application section, which applies the results of the "Relationship Test" to a practical exercise of Scripture memory and prayer.

# WORKBOOK SECTION

Jesus came to reveal the heavenly Father, and the purpose of this study is to reinforce this truth in your own mind so that you might enjoy the benefits which are yours as a child of God.

1.   In John 10:30, what did Jesus tell the Jews? _____

_____

2.   Read John 14:8. What was it that Phillip wanted to see? _____

_____

3.   Read John 14:9-10. What was Jesus' reply to Phillip? _____

_____

4.   Read John 14:6. How can we come to know the Father? _____

_____

5.   Read John 5:18. Why were the Jews trying to kill Jesus? _____

_____

6.   Read John 5:19. What was Jesus' statement concerning what He said and did? _____

_____

7.   Read John 5:43. In whose name did Jesus come? _____

8.   In John 8:58, Jesus refers to Himself as the "I AM." Read Exodus 3:14 and comment on the connection. What was Jesus claiming to be?

_____

_____

9.   Read John 17:26. What did Jesus say that He came to do? _____

_____

10.   According to 2 Corinthians 6:18, what are we as Christians and who are we told that God is to us? _____

_____

11.   Explain Psalms 68:5 in your own words. Before you do, reread "The Need to Feel Secure" section of this booklet (p. 14). _____

_____

_____

12.   If God is a Father – a Father to us – we need to know some of the characteristics of God as Father. For example, Paul says in 2 Corinthians 1:3 that God our Father is the God of mercies and comfort. Therefore, two characteristics

of our Father are that He is merciful toward us and that He comforts us. From Psalm 3:3-5, list at least four characteristics of what God is to you as a Father. _____

_____

_____

13. According to Zephaniah 3:17, what is your Father's attitude toward you?

_____

14. In 1 John 4:10, what are you told is God's attitude toward you?

_____

In Romans 15:7? _____

15. Do you feel it is important to you to know God as your Father? Why or why not? _____

_____

_____

16. In the following passages, God is described by certain characteristics of a Father. For example, in 2 Corinthians 1:3, God is called the Father of mercies. Look up each passage and fill in the descriptive word or phrase that describes a characteristic of the Father.

Matthew 5:48: "... as your Heavenly Father is _____."

Matthew 6:18: "... your Father who sees in secret will _____
_____."

Luke 11:13: "... how much more shall your heavenly Father _____
_____?"

John 14:2-3: "In my Father's house _____."

John 16:23: "... if you shall ask the Father for anything, He _____
_____."

Romans 1:7b: "_____ from God our Father."

Romans 8:16: "The Spirit himself bears witness with our spirit that _____
_____."

2 Cor. 1:3b: "... the Father of _____
and God of _____."

Eph. 1:3: "Blessed be the God and Father of our Lord Jesus Christ, who has blessed us with _____
_____."

Eph. 1:17: "that the God of our Lord Jesus Christ, the _____

_____ may give to you _____

_____."

Eph. 3:14-19: "For this reason, I bow my knees before the _____

from whom every family in heaven and on earth derives its name, that He

would grant you, according to _____

to be _____

so that _____

_____

_____

_____

_____

_____."

James 1:17: "Every _____

is from above, coming down from _____

_____."

1 Peter 1:3: "Blessed is the _____

who according to His great mercy has _____

_____

_____."

# APPLICATION SECTION

# RELATIONSHIP TEST INSTRUCTIONS

This test is designed to allow you to rate your relationship with the heavenly Father. Because it is subjective, there are no wrong answers. To insure the test reveals your actual feelings, follow the instructions carefully.

1. To arrive at an accurate relationship rating, it is imperative that you answer openly and honestly. Do not answer the questions from a theological knowledge of God, but from a personal, experiential knowledge. Do not answer from what your relationship ought to be or what you hope it will be, but from what your relationship is with the Father right now. *In other words, if this test is to achieve its purpose, you must be absolutely candid in your answers.*

2. Some people feel that God might be displeased with them if they indicate a negative factor in answering the questions. Nothing could be further from the truth. Ask the Holy Spirit to guide you as you rate your relationship with the Father. He already knows how you feel and accepts you.

3. To guide you as you begin this test, you may find it helpful to phrase questions around each characteristic. For example, "To what degree do I really feel God loves me?" or "To what degree do I really know and experience God's majesty?" Your answers will form the subjective values that you assign each question.

4. It might be helpful to recall times of stress and difficulties as well as normal situations. *Who was God to you during these times?*

5. Moving from left to right, rate your relationship with the Father in terms of the degree to which each characteristic describes your experiential relationship with Him. *Rate yourself according to the following scale, circling the appropriate number that indicates your choice.*

## 1 - ALWAYS   2 - VERY OFTEN   3 - OFTEN   4 - SOMETIMES
## 5 - SELDOM   6 - HARDLY EVER   7 - NEVER

### AFTER THE TEST:

1. Wherever you have circled a "3" or higher, put an "X" in the column just to the left of the characteristic.

2. Once you have marked all the X's, transfer them to the corresponding columns in the FatherCare Bible study exercises that follow. There are ten characteris-

tics under each FatherCare heading. For each are listed verses and phrases which will help you in the "reparenting" process.

3. Choose a verse from among the key verses listed for each characteristic and begin to memorize the verse you choose. Establish a consistent prayer time when you can begin to pray out loud and choose to "put off" the wrong ideas about God and "put on" the right ideas about God. An example prayer is given at the end of this booklet. It is a good practice to write out your verses several times in longhand as well as to meditate on them.

# RELATIONSHIP TEST

## FatherCare:

| | |
|---|---|
| ____ Caring | 1 2 3 4 5 6 7 |
| ____ Loving | 1 2 3 4 5 6 7 |
| ____ Kind | 1 2 3 4 5 6 7 |
| ____ Understanding | 1 2 3 4 5 6 7 |
| ____ Strong | 1 2 3 4 5 6 7 |
| ____ Calm | 1 2 3 4 5 6 7 |
| ____ Pleasant | 1 2 3 4 5 6 7 |
| ____ Approving | 1 2 3 4 5 6 7 |
| ____ Sensitive | 1 2 3 4 5 6 7 |
| ____ Listens | 1 2 3 4 5 6 7 |

## FatherKing:

| | |
|---|---|
| ____ King | 1 2 3 4 5 6 7 |
| ____ Majestic | 1 2 3 4 5 6 7 |
| ____ Awesome | 1 2 3 4 5 6 7 |
| ____ Great | 1 2 3 4 5 6 7 |
| ____ Victorious | 1 2 3 4 5 6 7 |
| ____ Gracious | 1 2 3 4 5 6 7 |
| ____ Honorable | 1 2 3 4 5 6 7 |
| ____ Just | 1 2 3 4 5 6 7 |
| ____ Good | 1 2 3 4 5 6 7 |
| ____ Righteous | 1 2 3 4 5 6 7 |

## FatherSavior:

| | |
|---|---|
| ____ Redeemer | 1 2 3 4 5 6 7 |
| ____ Merciful | 1 2 3 4 5 6 7 |
| ____ Forgiving | 1 2 3 4 5 6 7 |
| ____ Compassionate | 1 2 3 4 5 6 7 |
| ____ Gentle | 1 2 3 4 5 6 7 |
| ____ Beautiful | 1 2 3 4 5 6 7 |
| ____ Cleanses | 1 2 3 4 5 6 7 |
| ____ Holy | 1 2 3 4 5 6 7 |
| ____ Pardons | 1 2 3 4 5 6 7 |
| ____ Reasonable | 1 2 3 4 5 6 7 |

## FatherFriend:

| | |
|---|---|
| ____ Friend | 1 2 3 4 5 6 7 |
| ____ Faithful | 1 2 3 4 5 6 7 |
| ____ Patient | 1 2 3 4 5 6 7 |
| ____ Delightful | 1 2 3 4 5 6 7 |
| ____ Truthful | 1 2 3 4 5 6 7 |
| ____ Counselor | 1 2 3 4 5 6 7 |
| ____ Supportive | 1 2 3 4 5 6 7 |
| ____ Humble | 1 2 3 4 5 6 7 |
| ____ Joyful | 1 2 3 4 5 6 7 |
| ____ Discerning | 1 2 3 4 5 6 7 |

## FatherProvider:

| | |
|---|---|
| ____ Provider | 1 2 3 4 5 6 7 |
| ____ Trustworthy | 1 2 3 4 5 6 7 |
| ____ Adequate | 1 2 3 4 5 6 7 |
| ____ Generous | 1 2 3 4 5 6 7 |
| ____ Fair | 1 2 3 4 5 6 7 |
| ____ Steadfast | 1 2 3 4 5 6 7 |
| ____ Wealthy | 1 2 3 4 5 6 7 |
| ____ Concerned | 1 2 3 4 5 6 7 |
| ____ Satisfies | 1 2 3 4 5 6 7 |
| ____ Giver | 1 2 3 4 5 6 7 |

## FatherProtector:

| | |
|---|---|
| ____ Protective | 1 2 3 4 5 6 7 |
| ____ Secure | 1 2 3 4 5 6 7 |
| ____ Preserver | 1 2 3 4 5 6 7 |
| ____ Alert | 1 2 3 4 5 6 7 |
| ____ Deliverer | 1 2 3 4 5 6 7 |
| ____ Defender | 1 2 3 4 5 6 7 |
| ____ Cherishes | 1 2 3 4 5 6 7 |
| ____ Advocate | 1 2 3 4 5 6 7 |
| ____ Forceful | 1 2 3 4 5 6 7 |
| ____ Courageous | 1 2 3 4 5 6 7 |

*FatherLove:*

____ Loving           1 2 3 4 5 6 7
____ Considerate      1 2 3 4 5 6 7
____ Comforting       1 2 3 4 5 6 7
____ Encouraging      1 2 3 4 5 6 7
____ Lover            1 2 3 4 5 6 7
____ Accepting        1 2 3 4 5 6 7
____ Intimate         1 2 3 4 5 6 7
____ Pleasing         1 2 3 4 5 6 7
____ Rewarder         1 2 3 4 5 6 7
____ Appreciative     1 2 3 4 5 6 7

*FatherLeader:*

____ Guide            1 2 3 4 5 6 7
____ Bold             1 2 3 4 5 6 7
____ Confident        1 2 3 4 5 6 7
____ Perfect          1 2 3 4 5 6 7
____ Devoted          1 2 3 4 5 6 7
____ Commander        1 2 3 4 5 6 7
____ Authoritative    1 2 3 4 5 6 7
____ Loyal            1 2 3 4 5 6 7
____ Sufficient       1 2 3 4 5 6 7
____ Decisive         1 2 3 4 5 6 7

*FatherTeacher:*

____ Instructor       1 2 3 4 5 6 7
____ Wise             1 2 3 4 5 6 7
____ Creative         1 2 3 4 5 6 7
____ Helpful          1 2 3 4 5 6 7
____ Lovingly Kind    1 2 3 4 5 6 7
____ Disciplines      1 2 3 4 5 6 7
____ Hopeful          1 2 3 4 5 6 7
____ Favor            1 2 3 4 5 6 7
____ Light            1 2 3 4 5 6 7
____ Respectful       1 2 3 4 5 6 7

# FATHERCARE – THE CHARACTERISTICS OF THE FATHER

As you do each of the following studies, ask yourself these questions:

1.  Does this passage clearly support the point made in the characteristic?
2.  Are there any cross references which might better highlight or emphasize that characteristic?
3.  Have I personally had an experience with God in which this trait was made clear to me? If not, do I have trouble believing God is this way?

    If you do have trouble in this area, write out a sentence prayer asking God to reveal this trait to you in some concrete situation. For example, with the trait "God is pleasant": "Lord, I ask you to reveal your pleasantness to me in my prayers—lately I've felt bored and dull when I pray."
4.  As I meditate upon this trait in God's character, what emotions come to the surface and what do they tell me about the condition of my belief system?
5.  How does this characteristic motivate me to greater love for God Himself rather than just to "serve in His name" or to see His gifts?

When you conclude each Bible study, write out a prayer to God, thanking Him for who He is and for how He has shown Himself to you and asking Him to continue to reveal Himself to you as the perfect Father He is. There is a sample prayer on the last page of this section.

**NOTE:**     Unless indicated otherwise, the Scripture references in this study are based on the wording in the New American Standard Version of the Bible. Wording may vary slightly in other translations.

*FatherCare:*

1. **Caring**: Matthew 6:26; 1 Peter 5:7
   ____ He cares for me as only a loving father can care for his child.
   ____ He not only cares for me, but He cares about me.
2. **Loving**: John 3:16; Romans 5:8; Ephesians 3:14-19
   ____ He loves me for who I am, not for what I do
   ____ His love for me is unconditional and unceasing.
3. **Kind**: Psalm 103:13; Romans 2:4; Ephesians 1:5
   ____ Our Father is a kind and considerate Person to us, His children.
   ____ He always has a kind and encouraging word for me.
4. **Understanding**: Psalm 103:14; 139:1; Hebrews 4:15
   ____ My Father understands me as a person.
   ____ He understands me in my moods, my feelings, my thoughts, my actions.
5. **Strong**: Psalm 93:1; 105:4; 106:8; Ephesians 6:10-13
   ____ My Father is strong and powerful on my behalf.
   ____ His strength becomes my strength. He is the strongest of the strong.
6. **Calm**: Psalm 37:7; Matthew 11:28; John 14:1
   ____ I find my tranquility in my Father's calmness. He is never hurried or harassed.
   ____ He calms the anxious heart and takes senseless activity and turns it into creative productivity.
7. **Pleasant**: Psalm 16:11; 21:6; 147:1
   ____ My Father is absolutely pleasant. What a pleasure it is to be in His presence.
   ____ He is altogether lovely.
8. **Approving**: John 6:27 with Colossians 3:3
   ____ My Father gives me unconditional approval.
   ____ His approval is based on who I am in Him and not on what I do or have.
9. **Sensitive**: Psalm 94:9; 139:1-6, 17-18; Hebrews 4:15
   ____ My Father is sensitive to my every mood and thought.
   ____ He is sensitive to my needs and desires.
10. **Listens**: Psalm 55:17; 102:17; 116:1-2
    ____ My Father listens to me. He takes time to be involved in who I am and what I do.
    ____ He knows what I have to say is important. It is important to me; therefore, it is important to Him.

*FatherKing:*

1. **King**: Psalm 47:7; 95:3
   - \_\_\_\_ My Father is the sovereign king of the whole universe. He is the Kind Most High!
   - \_\_\_\_ I am a child of the King (John 1:12). I am a prince/princess. He enables me to think as a child of the King, act as a child of the King, be the child of a King.
2. **Majestic**: 1 Chronicles 29:11-13; Psalm 93:1
   - \_\_\_\_ My Father is majestic. He rules and reigns on high. How great He is!
   - \_\_\_\_ He desires my participation in His majesty. He freely shares it all with me.
3. **Awesome**: Exodus 15:11; Psalm 99:3
   - \_\_\_\_ My Father is awesome in His ability to love and protect me.
   - \_\_\_\_ He is awesome in His strength, power and holiness.
4. **Great**: Psalm 86:10; 99:2
   - \_\_\_\_ Greatness Becomes my Father. He is before all things, above all things; He presides over all things.
   - \_\_\_\_ He makes me an integral part of His greatness. I find my greatness in Him.
5. **Victorious:** Psalm 98:1; Zephaniah 3:17
   - \_\_\_\_ My Father is victorious over all things – the world, the flesh and the devil.
   - \_\_\_\_ His victory allows me to be victorious.
6. **Gracious:** Psalm 86:15; 111:4; 119:132; Ephesians 1:7-8
   - \_\_\_\_ He is gracious to me no matter how I act toward Him.
   - \_\_\_\_ He lavishes His grace on me as His precious child.
7. **Honorable:** Philippians 2:9; 1 Timothy 6:15-16
   - \_\_\_\_ My Father is distinguished and upright. His name is above every other name.
   - \_\_\_\_ I am so very proud of Him. I am proud to call Him Father.
8. **Just:** Deuteronomy 32:4; Psalm 89:14; 99:4
   - \_\_\_\_ My Father is absolutely just. I know that He is impartial.
   - \_\_\_\_ I know that He will be just with me no matter what.
9. **Good:** Psalm 34:8; 100:5; 106:1
   - \_\_\_\_ My Father is good, a good Person in every sense.
   - \_\_\_\_ He is so good to me. He insists on giving me everything out of the goodness of His heart.
10. **Righteous:** Deuteronomy 32:4; Psalm 11:7; 111:3; 119:137
    - \_\_\_\_ My Father is absolutely righteous, even though He had been tempted in every manner just like me.
    - \_\_\_\_ Because He is righteous, He has made me to be righteous, not because of what I do, but because of who I am in Him.

*FatherSavior:*

1. **Redeemer:** Psalm 19:14; Isaiah 63:16; Jeremiah 50:34
   ____ My Father cared enough to redeem me out of the authority of darkness.
   ____ He redeemed me from the power of sin and from the hold of Satan, and He put me into His kingdom.
2. **Merciful:** 2 Samuel 24:14; Psalm 86:15; Ephesians 2:4
   ____ My Father is always merciful to me, regardless of my circumstances.
   ____ In the dark storms of self-reproach and condemnation, He is always merciful.
3. **Forgiving:** Psalm 86:5; 103:10-12; Hebrews 10:17
   ____ He has forgiven me completely and totally for all my sins and transgressions, past, present and future.
   ____ He forgives, He forgets – He wipes the slate of my heart clean.
4. **Compassionate:** Psalm 103:8, 13; 111:4; Matthew 9:36
   ____ My Father's heart is full of compassion for me for He has shared intimately all my pain and hurt and sorrows.
   ____ Through His compassion, He affirms and supports me.
5. **Gentle:** Psalm 18:35; Matthew 11:29; 21:5
   ____ He is a gentle Person. He deals with me so gently.
   ____ My Father's gentleness permeates my being, making me a gentle person.
6. **Beautiful:** Psalm 27:4; 96:6
   ____ He is the lily of the valley, the bright and morning star, the fairest of ten thousand.
   ____ My Father is a beautiful Person, and He believe me to be a beautiful person.
7. **Cleanses:** Isaiah 1:18; Acts 15:9; 1 John 1:9
   ____ The blood of Christ cleanses me from all unrighteousness.
   ____ No matter the defilement, my Father cleanses, moment by moment.
8. **Holy:** Psalm 99:3, 5, 9; 108:7
   ____ The beauty of holiness shrouds my Father.
   ____ He is absolutely holy, thus He makes me holy.
9. **Pardons:** Psalm 103:3; Romans 8:1; Hebrews 10:17
   ____ He freely pardons me – all my sins, all my transgressions; even the defilement is pardoned. I am free.
   ____ The Father took me as His precious child and sacrificed His Son to pardon me.
10. **Reasonable:** Isaiah 1:18; 1 Corinthians 10:13
    ____ To think that my Father would reason with me. How important that makes me feel.
    ____ He never demands more than I am able to really give. In every way, He is so very reasonable.

*FatherFriend:*

1. **Friend:** John 15:13-15
   ____ My Father is my friend. He is closer than a brother.
   ____ Since He is my friend, I can call on Him at any time; He is never too busy for me.
2. **Faithful:** Numbers 23:19; Psalm 89:1,2,5,8; 100:5; Lamentations 3:23-24
   ____ My Father is absolutely faithful to me as a person.
   ____ His faithfulness to me never lags and will never end.
3. **Patient:** Psalm 86:15: 103:8; 1 Corinthians 13:4
   ____ My Father is so patient with me. Nothing affects His patience where it concerns me.
   ____ I cannot provoke Him, nor does He ever hold anything against me.
4. **Delightful:** Psalm 18:19; 27:4; Zephaniah 3:17
   ____ My Father delights in me because I am me; that is enough for Him.
   ____ He is a delightful and pleasing Person.
5. **Truthful:** Psalm 86:15; 89:14; 108:4; John 14:6
   ____ My Father is always truthful to me, to everyone. He cannot be untruthful.
   ____ He builds into me truthfulness. I can be truthful because He is truthful.
6. **Counselor:** Job 12:13; Psalm 73:24; Proverbs 19:21; Isaiah 9:6
   ____ There is nothing that I cannot bring before my Father and seek His counsel on.
   ____ He never condemns or belittles what I ask Him. His advice never fails.
7. **Supportive:** Psalm 37:23-24; Isaiah 41:10
   ____ My Father supports and cares for me.
   ____ I know that whatever I attempt, He is there. What He requires of me, He give me the strength and power to do.
8. **Humble:** Matthew 11:29; Philippians 2:6-11
   ____ To think that the King of kings humbled Himself for me.
   ____ Out of my Father's humbleness, I find my humility.
9. **Joyful:** Isaiah 62:5; Zephaniah 3:17; John 15:11
   ____ My Father is always joyful and full of joy. He is a Father of joy.
   ____ His joy for me and in me produces my joy. I can rejoice in Him.
10. **Discerning:** 1 Samuel 16:7; Jeremiah 17:10; Mark 2:8
    ____ My Father is so very discerning. He knows my heart and nothing is hidden from Him.
    ____ I can be myself. I don't have to be a phony since He knows my heart.

*FatherProvider:*

1. **Provider:** Psalm 23; Isaiah 58:11; Matthew 6:25-34; Philippians 4:19
   - ____ My Father provides for my every need – emotional, spiritual and physical.
   - ____ I can rest secure knowing that He will provide for me as He has promised.
2. **Trustworthy:** Psalm 9:10; 18:2; 65:5; 2 Corinthians 1:20
   - ____ In every way, in every circumstance of life, my Father is trustworthy.
   - ____ He is worthy of the trust I place in Him.
3. **Adequate:** 1 Chronicles 29:12; Psalm 73:25-28; 2 Corinthians 3:5
   - ____ My Father is totally adequate for all my needs. He is, in and of Himself, totally adequate.
   - ____ His adequacy is the basis for my own personal adequacy. My adequacy is in and of Him.
4. **Generous:** Matthew 7:9-11; John 3:34; Romans 8:32; Philippians 4:19
   - ____ My Father withholds nothing good from me. He lavishes the riches of His grace upon me.
   - ____ He freely and bountifully gives me all good things.
5. **Fair:** Deuteronomy 32:4; Psalm 98:9; 99:4
   - ____ How fair in all of His dealings with me is my Father.
   - ____ I know that He will never, ever be unfair with me.
6. **Steadfast:** Psalm 31:3; Isaiah 40:8; 2 Thessalonians 3:5; Hebrews 13:8
   - ____ What security I can have because my Father is steadfast and unmovable.
   - ____ He is like a rock; I can truly trust Him.
7. **Wealthy:** Psalm 50:10; 2 Corinthians 8:9
   - ____ My Father owns the cattle on a thousand hills. He is rich beyond comprehension. His wealth is my wealth right now as my present possession.
   - ____ My Father's real wealth is me. I am His inheritance.
8. **Concerned:** Matthew 6:28-32; 10:29-31; 1 Peter 5:7
   - ____ My Father is deeply concerned with the intimate details of my life.
   - ____ I can trust Him because He cares about me.
9. **Satisfies:** Psalm 103:5; 107:9; 128:1-4; 147:14
   - ____ In my Father I am fulfilled.
   - ____ He satisfies beyond my wildest dreams.
10. **Giver:** Psalm 37:4; John 3:34; Romans 8:32; James 1:17
    - ____ No good thing does my Father withhold from me, His child.
    - ____ He brings gifts and gives them to me – the gift of the Sprit, spiritual gifts and material blessings.

*FatherProtector:*

1. **Protective:** Psalm 91; 118:6-9; 2 Thessalonians 3:3
   ____ My Father protects me because He loves me.
   ____ As His precious child, He protects me.
2. **Secure:** Psalm 18:2; Proverbs 3:25-26; 29:25; Hebrews 13:8
   ____ In an insecure world, my Father gives me security.
   ____ The world offers no sanctuary of security; that only comes in Him.
3. **Preserver:** Psalm 97:10; 119:114; Isaiah 54:17: John 10:29
   ____ My Father preserves me and keeps me from all harm.
   ____ He maintains (preserves) His righteousness in me.
4. **Alert:** 2 Chronicles 16:9; Psalm 121:3-4: 139:1-12
   ____ If His eye is on the sparrow, then I know He watches me.
   ____ My Father watches over me even in the night watches. I am never alone.
5. **Deliverer:** Psalm 97:10; 107:6; 1 Corinthians 10:13
   ____ My Father delivers me from the hand of the enemy.
   ____ He delivers me from all temptation.
6. **Defender:** Psalm 10:18; 27:1; 108:13; Zechariah 9:15
   ____ My Father protects and defends me from myself and my enemies.
   ____ He stands up for me and is a shield to me.
7. **Cherishes:** Psalm 18:19; Zephaniah 3:17; Ephesians 5:29
   ____ My Father delights in me.
   ____ He cherishes me as a person dear to His heart.
8. **Advocate:** Hebrews 7:25; 1 John 2:1
   ____ My Father speaks up for me and defends me.
   ____ He proclaims to Satan that I am "not guilty."
9. **Forceful:** Isaiah 40:10-26; Mark 10:27; Luke 1:37
   ____ My Father accomplishes with ease that which man finds impossible.
   ____ He forcefully conquers His enemies and mine.
10. **Courageous:** Psalm 24:8; Acts 14:3; 1 Thessalonians 2:2; 2 Timothy 1:7
    ____ My Father courageously faces the foe on my behalf. I need not fear anything.
    ____ He builds courage in me. In Him I find that courage is not the absence of fear, but the victory over it.

*FatherLove:*

1. **Loving:** 1 Corinthians 13:4-8; 1 John 4:9-10
   ____ My Father is altogether loving. He is full of love.
   ____ He inspires love and affection in me.
2. **Considerate:** Psalm 139:17-18 (NIV—see marginal note); Isaiah 54:4-7;
   Jeremiah 29:11
   ____ My Father is so considerate of me. Even when I am wrong, His consideration does not change.
   ____ He never neglects nor ignores me. To Him I am so very important and special.
3. **Comforting:** Psalm 68:5; 94:19; 2 Corinthians 1:3-4
   ____ He comforts me in all the trials and tragedies I face.
   ____ My Father's comfort extends even to the most intimate areas of my life. There is nothing I can't share with Him.
4. **Encouraging:** Isaiah 35:2-4; 40:31; Romans 15:4-5
   ____ My Father encourages me constantly.
   ____ No matter what I face, the pain I feel, the hurt I experience, He is always encouraging me.
5. **Lover:** Romans 5:8; Ephesians 2:4; 3:17-19
   ____ He is the lover of my soul. He tenderly watches over and cares for me.
   ____ I am secure and confident in my Father's aggressive, yet tender, love for me.
6. **Accepting:** Romans 14:3-4; 15:7
   ____ My Father accepts me as a person, with all my hang-ups, all my sins, all my guilt. He accepts me just as I am.
   ____ He accepts me on the basis of who I am, not on the basis of what I do.
7. **Intimate:** Psalm 139; Proverbs 3:32; John 17:23
   ____ My Father is not someone who is ten million light years away; He is with me at all times.
   ____ He is not vague, but real. He is someone who does care and love.
8. **Pleasing:** Psalm 23:6; Matthew 11:28-30; John 1:14; Philippians 2:13
   ____ What a pleasing Person my Father is. His presence is like the radiance of the sun.
   ____ Not only does He try in every way to please me, but He makes me desire to please Him.
9. **Rewarder:** 2 Timothy 4:7-8; Hebrews 11:6; James 1:12
   ____ My Father has promised crowns to me.
   ____ Knowing Him intimately is reward enough in eternity.
10. **Appreciative:** Matthew 24:45-47; Luke 6:38; 2 Corinthians 9:6-11
   ____ My Father always shows His appreciation for my efforts on His behalf.
   ____ He appreciates me as a person.

*FatherLeader:*

1. **Guide:** Psalm 73:24; 107:30; Isaiah 58:11
   ___ I know, no matter what the call, my Father guides my way step by step.
   ___ His will is not elusive and will-o'-the-wisp, but a definite statement of His desires for me.
2. **Bold:** Psalm 76:3-9; Hebrews 4:16; Revelation 19:11-16
   ___ My Father is bold, bold for me.
   ___ He imparts boldness to me. He makes me to be bold.
3. **Confident:** Isaiah 41:13; 42:8; 45:5; 2 Corinthians 3:5
   ___ My Father is supremely confident. He knows what He is about.
   ___ Out of His confidence, He builds confidence in me.
4. **Perfect:** Deuteronomy 32:4; 2 Samuel 22:31 (NIV); Psalm 18:30 (NIV); Hebrews 7:28
   ___ Can anyone be as perfect as my Father? He is perfect in and of Himself. He is perfect to me.
   ___ He is the perfect Person for me, to make me everything that I could never be in and of myself.
5. **Devoted:** Hebrews 13:5-6; 1 John 3:1-2
   ___ My Father is devoted to me. He pours out His affection and love on me.
   ___ His devotion for me drove Him to the Cross. I am that worthy in His sight.
6. **Commander:** 2 Chronicles 13:12; Psalm 33:9; 47:3,9; Isaiah 55:4
   ___ My Father is the Commander of the host of the Lord.
   ___ He is in charge. Need I fear anything?
7. **Authoritative:** Matthew 7:29; 9:6; 10:1; 28:18
   ___ My Father speaks with authority.
   ___ He commands the attention and obedience of all.
8. **Loyal:** John 10:29; Romans 8:31-39; Hebrews 13:5
   ___ My Father's loyalty to me as His child never ceases.
   ___ He protects loyally. He never embarrasses nor humiliates me. He cares that I remain loyal and obedient to Him.
9. **Sufficient:** 2 Corinthians 9:8; 12:9-10
   ___ My Father is sufficient for every need, for every situation and circumstances of life.
   ___ His sufficiency guarantees that in my weakness His strength will be made perfect.
10. **Decisive:** Psalm 33:9; 2 Corinthians 1:18-20
    ___ My Father is decisive. He speaks and it is done.
    ___ He knows where He is going and how to get there. My indecision is to be swallowed up in His decisiveness.

*Father Teacher:*

1. **Instructor:** Psalm 25:8-9; 32:8; John 14:26; 2 Timothy 3:16-17
   ____ My Father carefully, patiently instructs me in everything.
   ____ He prepares me fully to live a life for Him.
2. **Wise:** Job 9:4; 12:13; Psalm 104:24; Romans 16:27; James 1:5
   ____ My Father is wise beyond imagination. I cannot fathom His wisdom, but it is always the best for me.
   ____ He imparts His wisdom to me, so that I might be truly wise.
3. **Creative:** Psalm 102:25; 104:1-24; John 1:3; Ephesians 2:10; 2 Corinthians 5:17
   ____ In His creative genius, He carefully fashions all that is.
   ____ My Father created me twice – once in His image, and again in spirit.
4. **Helpful:** Psalm 10:14; 54:4; 121:1-2; John 14:16; Hebrews 13:6
   ____ My Father is my Helper.
   ____ What I find impossible in my own strength, I find possible in His.
5. **Lovingly Kind:** Psalm 25:6; 86:5; 89:1; 103:10-14
   ____ My Father's loving kindness is constantly extended toward me.
   ____ His loving kindness forms a shield over me, a guard in front of me, a hedge behind me.
6. **Disciplines:** Psalm 94:12; Isaiah 30:20-21; Hebrews 12:5-11; Revelation 3:19
   ____ My Father will not allow me to stray into danger.
   ____ He tenderly corrects me so that I may live life at its best.
7. **Hopeful:** Jeremiah 29:11; 33:3; Romans 15:4
   ____ My Father never gives up on me; He's always optimistic for me.
   ____ He gives me hope out of the great hope within Him.
8. **Favor:** Psalm 30:5; 89:17
   ____ I find my Father's favor in my intimacy with Him.
   ____ His favor suffices. It strengthens and keeps me.
9. **Light:** Psalm 4:6; 27:1; John 1:9; 8:12
   ____ My Father is the light of life, the light of the world.
   ____ In the darkness of my path of life, His light carefully guides my way.
10. **Respectful:** Job 1:8; 2:3; John 15:15; Hebrews 2:9-13
    ____ My Father respects me because He loves me as a person.
    ____ I don't have to earn His respect; He gives it to me freely.

# SAMPLE "REPARENTING" PRAYER

A prayer like the one that follows would be appropriate after each of the preceding Bible studies. In your prayer, acknowledge the characteristic of God that you now believe to be true according to His Word. This prayer is an example for the characteristic of "loving."

> **My Father, I always considered You an unloving God, but now I know that You are a *loving* Father to me. I choose now in faith to put off my false belief and I choose to believe that You are loving to me. I choose to believe what Your Word has to say about You rather than my feelings or reason or past experiences, and I know that Your Word says that You love me as a person and that your love is not based on my performance or on what I have or achieve. Thank You, my Father, for loving me unconditionally.**

# ABOUT THE AUTHOR

Jim Craddock came to Christ through the ministry of the Navigators while stationed in Okinawa during the Korean War. After graduating from the University of Colorado, he joined Campus Crusade for Christ, where he ministered for 15 years on campuses, as an area director, and as a conference speaker, frequently emphasizing the character and trustworthiness of the heavenly Father. In 1973, Jim founded Scope Ministries International in Oklahoma City, where he was a pioneer in Biblical counseling and a mentor to many others in that field. In 2005, Jim founded Global Training Network, where he taught, counseled, and authored over 35 books and booklets. Since his death in 2014, Jim's wife and lifelong ministry partner, Doris, and their daughter Christi continue their ministry under its current name, His Truth Transforms.

Made in the USA
San Bernardino, CA
11 November 2015